# Children's Authors

# J.R.R. Tolkien

Jill C. Wheeler
**ABDO Publishing Company**

## visit us at
## www.abdopublishing.com

Published by ABDO Publishing Company, 8000 West 78th Street, Edina, Minnesota 55439.
Copyright © 2009 by Abdo Consulting Group, Inc. International copyrights reserved in all countries. No part of this book may be reproduced in any form without written permission from the publisher. The Checkerboard Library™ is a trademark and logo of ABDO Publishing Company.

Printed in the United States.

Cover Photo: © Estate of Pamela Chandler/National Portrait Gallery, London
Interior Photos: Alamy p. 9; Getty Images pp. 5, 13, 15, 17, 19, 21; iStockphoto pp. 7, 11

Editors: Tamara L. Britton, Megan M. Gunderson
Art Direction: Neil Klinepier

### Library of Congress Cataloging-in-Publication Data

Wheeler, Jill C., 1964-
  J.R.R. Tolkien / Jill C. Wheeler.
     p. cm. -- (Children's authors)
  Includes bibliographical references and index.
  ISBN 978-1-60453-080-3
 1. Tolkien, J. R. R. (John Ronald Reuel), 1892-1973--Juvenile literature. 2. Authors, English--20th century--Biography--Juvenile literature. 3. Fantasy fiction, English--History and criticism--Juvenile literature. 4. Middle Earth (Imaginary place)--Juvenile literature. I. Title.

PR6039.O32Z893 2009
828'.91209--dc22
  [B]
                                        2008004804

# Contents

# Word Magician

J.R.R. Tolkien was a master magician. He worked magic with words! Tolkien started writing stories when he was about seven years old. Just a few years later, he began inventing languages.

Eventually, Tolkien began to write a **mythology**. It took place in a land he called Middle-earth. Tolkien set his book *The Hobbit* in this mythical land. Children loved *The Hobbit*. They wanted more stories about hobbits and Middle-earth.

Tolkien wrote *The Lord of the Rings* as a **sequel** to *The Hobbit*. Some literary **critics** consider it the greatest fantasy work ever written. It has fascinated more than 100 million readers since its publication in 1954. In the early 2000s, three movies based on the book earned a remarkable 17 **Academy Awards**.

Tolkien did not plan on writing children's books. He was a busy university professor. He also had a wife and four children. More than 70 years have passed since Tolkien wrote *The Hobbit*. Today, readers of all ages still enjoy his work.

It took Tolkien 12 years to write *The Lord of the Rings*. The book has been translated into 25 languages.

# Early Years

John Ronald Reuel Tolkien was born on January 3, 1892, in Bloemfontein, South Africa. He was called Ronald. His father, Arthur Tolkien, was a banker. His mother, Mabel Suffield Tolkien, took care of the house. Ronald had a younger brother named Hilary Arthur Reuel Tolkien.

Ronald's parents had moved to South Africa from England. At the time, gold and diamond mines made South Africa's **economy** strong. Arthur believed he could advance his career faster there than in England. He obtained a position at the Bank of Africa. Arthur was very happy.

Mabel did not like South Africa as much as her husband did. She did not like the climate, and she missed her family. Mabel looked forward to returning to England for a visit. In April 1895, she and the boys left Bloemfontein for Birmingham, England. Arthur planned to come later.

Mabel and her sons enjoyed their visit. They looked forward to Arthur's arrival. However, Arthur became ill with **rheumatic fever**. He died on February 15, 1896, before he could join his family in England. He was buried in Bloemfontein.

*A photograph of the cemetery in Bloemfontein taken near the time of Arthur's death.*

# A New Life

Mabel Tolkien found herself a widow with two small children and not much money. She and the boys moved to the small village of Sarehole. There, Ronald and Hilary played in the English countryside. Mabel taught them at home.

The boys studied many subjects, including Latin and French. Ronald liked learning Latin. He became interested in words. Ronald began to notice other languages, such as Welsh.

In 1900, the family moved back to Birmingham. It was time for Ronald to start school. He entered King Edward's School that September.

At King Edward's, Ronald was active in clubs and on sports teams. His favorite subjects were languages and literature. He admitted he studied Welsh and English when he should have studied Latin and Greek. Sometimes Ronald did not do well in other classes because he loved studying languages so much!

*Opposite page: Ronald and Hilary often played in the yard at this grain mill in Sarehole. One man who worked there was often covered in white flour. The boys called him the White Ogre!*

While at King Edward's, Ronald began inventing his own languages. He took inspiration from several languages that no one spoke anymore. They included Old English, Middle English, and Gothic.

But tragedy soon struck the family again. Mabel became very ill. She learned she had **diabetes**. At that time, doctors did not have **insulin** to treat the disease. Mabel died on November 14, 1904.

# True Love

Mabel had joined the Catholic Church in 1900. In her will, she named the family priest as Ronald and Hilary's guardian. The priest, Father Francis Morgan, helped pay Ronald's **tuition** at King Edward's.

For a while, the boys lived with a distant aunt. But eventually, Father Morgan placed them in a boarding house. One of the house's residents was a talented pianist named Edith Bratt. Ronald began spending time with her. Soon they fell in love.

Father Morgan found out about the relationship. He asked Ronald to stop seeing Edith. Father Morgan wanted Ronald to concentrate on his schoolwork. He said Ronald could contact Edith again when he was 21 years old. Ronald respected Father Morgan. So, he agreed.

Ronald focused on his schoolwork and prepared for university. In December 1909, he took the **scholarship** examination. But Ronald's neglect of his studies made a difference. He did not pass the test.

In December 1910, Ronald took the examination once again. This time he passed! He planned to study **philology** and languages at Exeter College at the University of Oxford, England.

As soon as he turned 21, Ronald wrote to Edith. She told him she was engaged to marry someone else. Ronald went to see Edith. He convinced her to marry him instead. They were married on March 22, 1916.

*Exeter College at the University of Oxford*

# Into the Trenches

**World War I** had started in 1914. Many Oxford University students left school to join the military. However, Tolkien had signed up for a program that allowed him to finish school before reporting for service. He graduated in 1915 with a **degree** in English language and literature.

On June 4, 1916, Tolkien left to join the war. The army took advantage of his talent for language. Tolkien trained in **Morse code** and a communication system that used flags. He also trained pigeons to deliver messages. However, Tolkien spent most of his time in trenches dug deep into the ground.

Tolkien caught **trench fever** just four months into his military service. He was forced to return to England for treatment. While Tolkien was recovering, he and Edith had their first child. John was born in 1917.

During this time, Tolkien began writing a **mythology**. He used his knowledge of stories and ancient languages to create a magical world he called Middle-earth. It had its own languages, people, and landscape.  He called this work *The Book of Lost Tales*.

*The Lancashire Fusiliers prepare their weapons before leaving the trenches during the Battle of the Somme. Tolkien served in this regiment.*

# Professor Tolkien

The war was nearly over when Tolkien was well enough to return to Oxford. This time, he was looking for a job. He found a position on the staff of the New English Dictionary. Today, it is known as the Oxford English Dictionary. This was a perfect job for someone who loved to study words and where they come from.

Tolkien spent two years working on the dictionary. Then, a teaching position opened up at the University of Leeds in Leeds, England. Tolkien got the job. He began teaching Old and Middle English. Tolkien also taught other ancient languages such as **medieval** Welsh and Gothic. In 1920, Tolkien and Edith's second child was born. They named him Michael.

In 1924, their son Christopher was born. That same year, the University of Leeds promoted Tolkien. He became the university's youngest professor.

Tolkien liked the university. However, he did not like Leeds. It was a dirty, industrial city that was very different from

*At Oxford, Tolkien was a professor of Anglo-Saxon until 1945. Then he was a professor of English until 1959.*

Oxford. The next year, the University of Oxford offered him a professorship. He quickly accepted and moved his family back to Oxford.

# *The Hobbit*

For the next 34 years, Tolkien taught at the University of Oxford. His days were long and full. Tolkien taught classes and gave lectures at the university. He also taught students at his home.

Tolkien did not come from a wealthy family. So, he had to earn his own income. However, university professors did not make a lot of money. And by 1929, Tolkien and Edith had welcomed their daughter, Priscilla. Now, he had a wife and four children to support.

To earn extra money, Tolkien graded extra papers. One summer day, he came across a page that a student had left blank. On the page he wrote, "In a hole in the ground there lived a hobbit." Tolkien did not know where the word *hobbit* came from. It had just popped into his head!

Soon, Tolkien began making up stories about the hobbit. Later, he wrote down the hobbit's story in *The Hobbit*. Tolkien set the story in Middle-earth, the land from *The Book of Lost Tales*. Some of the same characters from that work also appear in *The Hobbit*.

Tolkien's schedule left little time for writing. He had to write late at night or early in the morning. Tolkien read parts of the **manuscript** to his children. He also shared it with a group of writers he belonged to called The Inklings. C.S. Lewis was a fellow Inkling. He and Tolkien were good friends. Lewis encouraged Tolkien to finish the book.

*C.S. Lewis wrote The Chronicles of Narnia series, among other works.*

# *The Lord of the Rings*

*The Hobbit* was published in September 1937. Children loved it! All 1,500 copies sold out before Christmas. Readers wanted more stories from Middle-earth. So did Tolkien's publisher, Stanley Unwin. Unwin asked Tolkien to write a **sequel** to *The Hobbit*.

Tolkien offered Unwin *The Book of Lost Tales*. He now called it *The Silmarillion*. Unwin thought the book was good. But, he wanted a story with hobbits in it. So, Tolkien began a new hobbit book.

Tolkien started many stories only to find that they did not work. He wrote and rewrote passages and changed characters and names. The story quickly became darker and more serious than *The Hobbit*.

In 1949, Tolkien finished the book. He called it *The Lord of the Rings*. Unwin decided the **manuscript** was too long to sell as a single book. He wanted to divide it into three books.

Tolkien disagreed. So, he offered the book to a different publisher. When that did not work out, he accepted Unwin's plan. *The Fellowship of the Ring* and *The Two Towers* were published in 1954. *The Return of the King* followed in 1955.

*Stanley Unwin started the George Allen and Unwin publishing house in 1914.*

# Writing to the End

*The Lord of the Rings* received mixed reviews. Some people loved it. Others found it confusing. In the 1960s, paperback editions became available. So, the series gained new interest, especially among college students. Soon, sales of *The Lord of the Rings* made Tolkien a wealthy man.

Tolkien retired from the University of Oxford in 1959. He and Edith moved to Bournemouth, England, a town by the sea. Tolkien continued to work on *The Silmarillion*. He also served as an editor of The Jerusalem Bible. Tolkien translated the book of Jonah from Hebrew into English. It was published in 1966.

Edith Tolkien died on November 29, 1971. Tolkien then returned to Oxford. In 1972, the university presented him with an honorary **doctorate**. Tolkien lived at the university until his death on September 2, 1973.

Tolkien's son Christopher completed *The Silmarillion*. It became the number one fiction best seller in fall 1977. That

**Opposite page:** *Tolkien wrote a story about a man named Beren who loved an elf named Lúthien. The elf gave up her magic to be with him. Tolkien always thought of Edith as his Lúthien.*

same year, an **animated** movie version of *The Hobbit* was released.

In 2001, *The Fellowship of the Ring* was released as a feature film. It won four **Academy Awards**. *The Two Towers* earned two Academy Awards in 2002. In 2003, *The Return of the King* won 11 Academy Awards. J.R.R. Tolkien enjoyed a lifelong love of words. His work remains popular today.

# Glossary

**Academy Award** - an award given by the Academy of Motion Picture Arts and Sciences to the best actors and filmmakers of the year.

**animation** - a process involving a projected series of drawings that appear to move due to slight changes in each drawing.

**critic** - a professional who gives his or her opinion on art, literature, or performances.

**degree** -  a title given by a college to its graduates after they have completed their studies.

**diabetes** - a disease in which a person's body cannot properly absorb normal amounts of sugar and starch.

**doctorate** - the highest graduate degree given by a university.

**economy** - the way a nation uses its money, goods, and natural resources.

**insulin** - a hormone, secreted by the pancreas, that regulates the body's use and storage of sugar and starch.  A preparation containing this hormone is used to treat diabetes.

**manuscript** - a book or an article written by hand or typed before being published.

**medieval** - of or belonging to the Middle Ages, which is a period of time from AD 500 to 1500.

**Morse code** - a code that uses dots and dashes, or long and short sounds, to represent letters of the alphabet, numbers, and punctuation marks.  It is named for inventor Samuel F.B. Morse.

**mythology** - a collection of myths from a certain group of people.

**philology** - the study of languages, especially their history and development.

**rheumatic fever** - a disease that occurs mainly in children. It is characterized by fever and pain in the joints and especially in the lungs.

**scholarship** - a gift of money to help a student pay for instruction.

**sequel** - a book or a movie continuing a story that began previously.

**trench fever** - a disease marked by fever and pain in the muscles, bones, and joints. It is caused by bacteria transmitted by body lice.

**tuition** - money students pay to receive instruction.

**World War I** - from 1914 to 1918, fought in Europe. Great Britain, France, Russia, the United States, and their allies were on one side. Germany, Austria-Hungary, and their allies were on the other side.

# Web Sites

To learn more about J.R.R. Tolkien, visit ABDO Publishing Company on the World Wide Web at **www.abdopublishing.com**. Web sites about J.R.R. Tolkien are featured on our Book Links page. These links are routinely monitored and updated to provide the most current information available.

# Index